SIT!

and take
a moment
with God

Devotions
*Best Enjoyed
in the Company
of a* Good Dog

*Inspired
by Faith*

Sit! and take a moment with God
©Product Concept Mfg., Inc.

Sit! and take a moment with God
ISBN 978-0-9828555-9-1

Published by Product Concept Mfg., Inc.
2175 N. Academy Circle #200, Colorado Springs, CO 80909

©2011 Product Concept Mfg., Inc. All rights reserved.

Sayings not having a credit listed are contributed by writers
for Product Concept Mfg., Inc. or in a rare case,
the author is unknown.

Written and Compiled by Patricia Mitchell
in association with Product Concept Mfg., Inc.

SIT!

and take
a moment
with God

Faithful friends and devoted companions, dogs quickly earn a special place in our hearts. *From the point of their velvet nose to the tip of their wagging tail, they bring unfeigned affection to their humans and complete dedication to the place they call home.*

Sit! highlights the fun and frolic, mishaps and happenings, antics and adventures that anyone who has ever loved a dog will recognize. Short biblically oriented reflections and classic quotations follow, readings designed to encourage and inspire you, move you forward in your spiritual life and bring you peace.

We invite you to Sit!—preferably with your canine buddy—and enjoy!

Do you want to go out and play? Shall we go for a walk? Want to ride along with me? Ask your dog, and you're guaranteed an instant tail-wagging Yes! You'll never hear excuses like "I'm too busy right now," or "Can we put that off until later?" It won't happen, because your dog loves to spend time with you.

Attentive to You

Yes! is the word you'll hear from God when you look for His presence and yearn for His attention. He is listening for the sound of your voice, and He's ready to respond to your needs and desires.

No matter where in your life you are right now, He's there for you, offering you His help and support, forgiveness and comfort, patience and kindness.

He would love to spend some time with you.

Dear God,
thank You for
saying Yes to me.
Amen

God loves each of us
as if there were only one of us.
Augustine

The LORD is nigh unto all
them that call upon him,
to all that call upon him in truth.
Psalm 145:18

That they should seek the Lord,
if haply they might feel after him,
and find him, though he be not
far from every one of us.
Acts 17:27

He is more within us
than we are ourselves.
Elizabeth Ann Seton

I am with you always,
even unto the end of the world.
Matthew 28:20

I take for my sureties:

The power of God to guide me,

The might of God to uphold me,

The wisdom of God to teach me,

The eye of God to watch over me,

The ear of God to hear me.

Prayer of St. Patrick

Throw the ball, and watch your dog run to fetch it. With his eyes on the ball, he runs like its echo, swerving neither right nor left. He nips the target before it touches the ground, dashes back to you, pulls to a halt, and lays it gently at your feet. His joyful eyes beg for another moment like this!

The Present Moment

With so many things going on at once, it's hard to focus on only one. In fact, some of us don't even try! Instead, we pride ourselves on being expert multi-taskers.

Multi-tasking lets us check items off our to-do list, but it doesn't help us find satisfaction in what we do. Satisfaction comes only when we give ourselves fully to the one thing we're doing this moment, whether in home or office, in church or community.

Today, discover the satisfaction of being in the present moment.

Help me live fully, dear God, in the present moment. Amen

Every second is of infinite value.
Johann von Goethe

Tomorrow's life is too late. Live today.
Martial

This is the day
which the LORD hath made;
we will rejoice and be glad in it.
Psalm 118:24

Whatsoever ye do, do it heartily,
as to the Lord.
Colossians 3:23

The dog has four feet, but he does not
walk in four roads at the same time.
English Proverb

Love the Lord thy God with all thy
heart, and with all thy soul,
and with all thy mind.
Matthew 22:37

Let me tell thee, time is a very precious
gift of God; so precious that it's only
given to us moment by moment.
Amelia Barr

To finish the moment, to find the journey's end in every step of the road, to live the greatest number of good hours, is wisdom.

Ralph Waldo Emerson

He is blessed over all mortals who loses no moment of the passing life in remembering the past.

Henry David Thoreau

A dog waits all day for the sound of her human's footsteps...for the click of the key in the lock... for the first glimpse of the familiar face, the proffered hand. Now it's bliss! Her companion is home, and at last she gets to pour out her warm and welcoming love.

Comfort with God

Difficult people, close deadlines, frustrating obstacles, unforeseen setbacks—all these and more make for a long and tiring day. Yet the day's worries and weariness slip away in the presence of home's warm, welcoming, accepting love.

No matter how your day has turned out, God opens His arms to comfort you with His renewing and life-giving love. Let go of your worries and anxieties, your disappointments and frustrations. Give each one to Him, because He has the strength to carry them all.

He's right here to welcome you.

Dear God,
renew and restore
me in Your love.
Amen

Come unto me, all ye that labour
and are heavy laden,
and I will give you rest.
Matthew 11:28

Until one has loved an animal
a part of one's soul remains unawakened.
Anatole France

They that wait upon the Lord
shall renew their strength;
they shall mount up with wings as eagles;
they shall run, and not be weary;
and they shall walk, and not faint.
Isaiah 40:31

It is possible that a man can be so-
changed by love as hardly to be
recognized as the same person.
Terence

'Tis sweet to hear the watch dog's honest bark
Bay deep-mouthed welcome as we draw near home;
'Tis sweet to know there is an eye will mark
Our coming and look brighter when we come.
Lord Byron

To live without loving is not really
to live.

Molière

The remedy of all blunders,
the cure of blindness, the cure
of crime, is love.

Ralph Waldo Emerson

He knows how to have fun wherever he is. Good natured whatever the weather, eager to explore everything that catches his eye (even though it was thoroughly sniffed just yesterday), frolicsome without fail, a dog is an A-one expert when it comes to knowing how to play!

Time to Play

Once we take on the responsibilities of adulthood, we tend to leave behind the pleasure of pure play. We don't have time... there's so much to do...and after all, isn't play just for kids?

Play is a gift God has given us, and He intends for play to season our lives with joy and laughter. It's what our body needs to release tension and stress, and it's what our spirit craves for renewal and rejuvenation.

Today, take time out to do something that has no other purpose than to make you laugh. You don't have to be under 12 (or a member of the canine family) to enjoy the blessing of play.

Dear God,
teach me to laugh...
teach me to play!
Amen

A happy heart
makes the face cheerful.
Proverbs 15:13 NIV

Is any merry? let him sing psalms.
James 5:13

If you want to be happy, be.
Leo Tolstoy

Joy is the holy fire that keeps
our purpose warm and our
intelligence aglow.
Helen Keller

You can discover more
about a person in an hour of play
than in a year of conversation.
Plato

The great pleasure of a dog is that you may
make a fool of yourself with him
and not only will he not scold you,
but he will make a fool of himself too.
Samuel Butler

Rejoice evermore.
1 Thessalonians 5:16

A merry heart doeth good
like a medicine.

Proverbs 17:22

Good work and joyous play go
hand in hand. When play stops,
old age begins. Play keeps you
from taking life too seriously.

Lord Byron

He doesn't mind when you tie a bow around his neck and exclaim what a handsome dog he is, and he sits still (more or less) in front of the camera while you record the moment for posterity. "You've got to tolerate them," his patient look explains. "After all, they're only human."

Gift of Tolerance

*Some people do the oddest things!
Yet after we learn more about their back-
ground, motivation, and goals, we often
discover that what they do makes sense.
Now that we know where they're coming
from, it's easy to accept their ways.*

*Toleration of others is even easier when
we remember that everyone's life comes
from God. We are one in humanity, one in
the world, one in the love of our Father.*

*Let your words and actions embody
tolerance toward those you meet today.*

Dear God,
grant me the gift of
tolerance for others.
Amen

If a profound gulf separates my
neighbor's belief from mine, there is
always the golden bridge of tolerance.

Author Unknown

Accept one another.

Romans 15:7 NIV

Love ye therefore the stranger: for ye
were strangers in the land of Egypt.

Deuteronomy 10:19

*Never judge a man until you have
walked a mile in his shoes.*

American Proverb

Judge not, and ye shall not be judged:
condemn not, and ye shall not
be condemned: forgive,
and ye shall be forgiven.

Luke 6:37

*The responsibility of tolerance lies
with those who have the wider vision.*

George Eliot

One man esteemeth one day above
another: another esteemeth every day
alike. Let every man be
fully persuaded in his own mind.

Romans 14:5

The best thing to give to your enemy is forgiveness; to an opponent, tolerance; to a friend, your heart; to your child, a good example; to a father, deference; to your mother, conduct that will make her proud of you; to yourself, respect; to all men, charity.

Benjamin Franklin

Clouds gather and dim the afternoon sunshine. Soon thunder's growl rumbles in the distance, and a flick of lightning strikes the sky. In the yard, the black dog stands to her full height, lifts her head to the sky, and howls her fierce displeasure.

Conquering Life's Storms

When life's storms appear on the horizon, our first reaction is to grumble about our bad luck. Yet complaints do nothing to turn away the storm!

God has promised His help at all times, especially those times that bring us face to face with setbacks, anxiety, or fear. He invites us to run under the umbrella of His wisdom and to seek the shelter of His love. Despite all the scary noises around us, we will be safe.

The storms of life are bigger than you are. Let God, whose power exceeds human imagination, see you through them.

Dear God,
let me find my
refuge in You.
Amen

The LORD is my rock, and my fortress,
and my deliverer.
Psalm 18:2

Bad times have a scientific value.
These are occasions a good learner
would not miss.
Ralph Waldo Emerson

Adversity is the first path to truth.
Lord Byron

Cowards falter, but danger is often
overcome by those who nobly dare.
Elizabeth I

He arose, and rebuked the wind, and said
unto the sea, Peace, be still. And the wind
ceased, and there was a great calm.
Mark 4:39

God is our refuge and strength, a very
present help in trouble.
Psalm 46:1

Every word of God is flawless; he is a shield
to those who take refuge in him.
Proverbs 30:5

Affliction is a treasure, and scarce is any man who hath enough of it. No man hath affliction enough that is not matured, and ripened by it, and made fit for God by that affliction.

John Donne

The LORD is my light and my salvation; whom shall I fear? the LORD is the strength of my life; of whom shall I be afraid?

Psalm 27:1

Taking care of a dog is a major commitment, because she depends on her human for food, shelter, and love. She needs time and attention every day for a healthy relationship to develop and endure. But the reward is beyond measure: her faithful and dependable love.

Commitment's Reward

*Living a spiritual life is a commitment.
If your goal is to spend more time in prayer
or meditation, then set aside a few minutes
each day for those practices. If you want
to get to know scriptures better, then even
a short daily reading will bring familiarity
and understanding.*

*Your commitment to spiritual growth
opens you to receive the rewards of God's
love and the peace that come with His
presence in your mind and heart.*

Lead me, God,
as I grow in love
for You.
Amen

Whatever I do,
I give up my whole self to it.
Edna Saint Vincent Millay

Let us not be weary in well doing.
Galatians 6:9

The middle of the road is where
the white line is —
and that's the worst place to drive.
Robert Frost

I am seeking, I am striving, I am in it
with all my heart.
Vincent van Gogh

Now I am steel-set: I follow the call to the
clear radiance and glow of the heights.
Henrik Ibsen

He did it with all his heart,
and prospered.
2 Chronicles 31:21

Always bear in mind that your own
resolution to succeed is more important
than any other one thing.
Abraham Lincoln

Whether therefore ye eat, or drink, or whatsoever ye do, do all to the glory of God.

1 Corinthians 10:31

Blessed are they that keep his testimonies, and that seek him with the whole heart.

Psalm 119:2

Quiet as a shadow, your dog slips into the dining room. He sits behind your chair, not making a sound. The aroma of your dinner is delectable to him, and even though he has been trained not to beg at the table, he can't resist. He moves to your side and rests his muzzle gently on your lap.

Necessary Boundaries

Most of us chafe against rules, yet we admit they're necessary. Imagine if there were no rules for drivers of automobiles or pilots of aircraft–the consequences would be disastrous!

God's rules for us keep us from the disastrous consequences of unwise choices and dangerous desires. Scriptures tell us "God is not the author of confusion, but of peace." If you feel unclear about God's rules... if there's one you're wondering about... turn to Him with a spirit of openness. Let His lovingly placed boundaries lead you into a closer relationship with Him.

Dear God, open to me
Your wisdom and increase
my understanding.
Amen

Incline thine ear unto wisdom,
and apply thine heart to understanding.
Proverbs 2:2

Don't ever take a fence down until you know
the reason it was put up.
G. K. Chesterton

The strength of man consists in finding out
the way in which God is going,
and going in that way too.
Henry Ward Beecher

True love grows by sacrifice and the more
thoroughly the soul rejects natural satisfaction
the stronger and more detached
its tenderness becomes.
Thérèse of Lisieux

The statutes of the LORD are right,
rejoicing the heart: the commandment
of the LORD is pure, enlightening the eyes.
Psalm 19:8

Resign every forbidden joy;
restrain every wish that is not
referred to God's will; banish all
eager desires, all anxiety. Desire
only the will of God; seek Him
alone, and you will find peace.

François Fénelon

It is God who works in you to
will and to act in order to fulfill
his good purpose.

Philippians 2:13 NIV

Given what she needs for her physical and emotional well-being, a dog is the picture of contentment. She doesn't care if the dog on the other side of the fence lives in a bigger dog house or struts down the street on a fancier leash. She has everything she needs right here, and she knows it.

Picture of Contentment

Surrounded as we are by ads, commercials, and come-ons begging us to update and upgrade, it's no wonder many of us feel discontent! It takes a conscious decision to curb our whims with an assessment of our real needs, our wants with a review of our financial resources.

The source of true contentment is gratitude—gratitude to God for what you have right now. Counting your blessings is a good way to start. Chances are, you'll get tired of counting long before you run out of blessings!

Thank You,
dear God, for
everything You have
given to me.
Amen

I have learned, in whatsoever state
I am, therewith to be content.
Philippians 4:11

No one can be poor that has enough, or
rich, that covets more than he has.
Seneca

A contented mind is the greatest
blessing a man can enjoy in this world.
Joseph Addison

Be content with such things as ye have:
for he hath said, I will never leave thee,
nor forsake thee.
Hebrews 13:5

Let us not be desirous of vain glory,
provoking one another,
envying one another.
Galatians 5:26

The fountain of contentment must spring up in the mind, and he who has so little knowledge of human nature as to seek happiness by changing anything but his own disposition, will waste his life in fruitless efforts and multiply the grief he proposes to remove.

Samuel Johnson

Godliness with contentment is great gain.

1 Timothy 6:6

A dog owns nothing, yet is seldom dissatisfied.

Irish Proverb

It's difficult to get a dog's focus off what engages him! Be it a squirrel scampering up a tree or leaves skittering across the lawn, he watches intently until he's good and ready to move on and discover something new.

Focused on God

With your spiritual eyes focused on God, expect to see marvelous things!

Only with the eyes of your spirit looking to Him will you notice the way He works in your day, comprehend the plans He has for your life, and perceive the depth of His love and compassion for you. Once you know what to watch for, you'll find clear evidence all around you.

Focus the eyes of your spirit on Him— you'll find a lot to look at!

God,
open the eyes
of my spirit to You.
Amen

As the eyes of servants look unto the
hand of their masters, and as the eyes
of a maiden unto the hand of her
mistress; so our eyes wait upon the
LORD our God.

Psalm 123:2

*Seek in reading and you will find in
meditation; knock in prayer and it will
be opened to you in contemplation.*

John of the Cross

I need nothing but God, and to lose
myself in the heart of Jesus.

Margaret Mary Alacoque

*O taste and see that the LORD is good:
blessed is the man that trusteth in him.*

Psalm 34:8

It is the heart which experiences God,
not the reason.

Blaise Pascal

*My voice shalt thou hear in the
morning, O LORD; in the morning
will I direct my prayer unto thee,
and will look up.*

Psalm 5:3

Many a humble soul will be amazed to find that the seed it sowed in weakness, in the dust of daily life, has blossomed into immortal flowers under the eyes of the Lord.

Harriet Beecher Stowe

Humans train some dogs to do a specific job, such as search and rescue; but most dogs provide training to their humans. A leash dangling from a muzzle and a scratch at the door has helped countless humans, for the sake of their beloved canines, to stick to their resolve to get some outside exercise every day!

Spiritual Fitness

As physical exercise benefits the body, spiritual exercise benefits the soul. Even five minutes of meditation each day relaxes your mind and keeps you in touch with your inmost self. Moments throughout the day given over to short, spontaneous prayer opens your spirit to God's strength, comfort, and encouragement.

Enjoy the divine privilege of keeping spiritually fit in God's love each day.

God, make me
eager to exercise
myself in You.
Amen

Exercise daily. Walk with the Lord!
Author Unknown

Seek those things which are above.
Colossians 3:1

Physical training is of some value,
but godliness has value for all things,
holding promise for both the present life and
the life to come.
1 Timothy 4:8 NIV

I would rather walk with God in the dark
than go alone in the light.
Mary Gardiner Brainard

The feeling remains
that God is on the journey, too.
Teresa of Avila

Lay up for yourselves treasures in heaven,
where neither moth nor rust doth corrupt.
Matthew 6:20

If you get to thinking you're a person
of some influence, try ordering
somebody else's dog around.
Cowboy Saying

We are not human beings having a spiritual experience. We are spiritual beings having a human experience.

Teilhard de Chardin

Put on the new man, which after God is created in righteousness and true holiness.

Ephesians 4:24

The majority of men live without being thoroughly conscious that they are spiritual beings.

Søren Kierkegaard

A chewed shoe...a raveled sock...telltale bite marks on the furniture—a dog's instincts get the better of him sometimes! Frequent reminders and gentle training help keep a dog's behavior in line with his human's needs and expectations.

Forgiveness Assured

Though we're aware of God's rules and expectations, we often do what we know we shouldn't...and neglect to do what we know we should. No one knows better than God how prone we are to succumb to temptation!

Never fear to approach God with your weaknesses, because He has no desire to punish. Instead, He promises to open His arms to you as you pour out your sorrow to Him, and He assures you of His forgiveness and continuing love and care.

Forgive me,
dear God, where I
have done wrong.
Amen

As far as the east is from the west, so far hath
he removed our transgressions from us.
Psalm 103:12

*He is a very green hand at life who cannot
forgive any mortal thing.*
Robert Lewis Stevenson

I have been all things unholy; if God can work
through me, he can work through anyone.
Francis of Assisi

*I want you to know that through Jesus the
forgiveness of sins is proclaimed to you.*
Acts 13:38 NIV

If ye forgive men their trespasses, your
heavenly Father will also forgive you.
Matthew 6:14

To err is human to forgive divine.
Alexander Pope

If we could read the secret history of our
enemies, we should find in each man's life
sorrow and suffering enough to
disarm hostility.
Henry Wadsworth Longfellow

*For thy name's sake, O LORD,
pardon mine iniquity; for it is great.*
Psalm 25:11

To make no mistake is not in the
power of man; but from their
errors and mistakes the wise and
good learn wisdom for the future.

Plutarch

I can forgive, but I cannot forget
is only another way of saying,
I will not forgive. Forgiveness
ought to be like a canceled note—
torn in two and burned up so that
it never can be shown against one.

Henry Ward Beecher

For some dogs, it's their crate; for others, it's a chair with their favorite blanket, or a corner of a room with their bed and a chew toy. All dogs need a place where they feel safe and secure...a special place they can call their own.

A Place of Peace

Where is your favorite place in the world? Whether it's across the country, across the globe, or right in the comfort of your own home, you like the way you feel when you're there.

God's favorite place to live is at the center of your heart. Invite Him in, and let Him bless you with His gift of inner peace and harmony. When you do, you may be surprised to find that the best of all places becomes wherever you happen to be!

Dear God,
grant me the gift
of inner peace.
Amen

Do not lose your inward peace for anything
whatsoever, even if your whole world seems upset.
Francis de Sales

The fruit of the Spirit is love, joy, peace...
Galatians 5:22

I learned that it is possible for us to create light,
sound and order within us no matter
what calamity may befall us in the outer world.
Helen Keller

Grace be to you and peace from God our Father,
and from the Lord Jesus Christ.
2 Corinthians 1:2

Peace I leave with you, my peace I give unto you.
John 14:27

Where there is peace and meditation,
there is neither anxiety nor doubt.
Francis of Assisi

The first step to bringing peace into the world is to
realize the peace that already dwells within you.
Author Unknown

First keep the peace within yourself,
then you can also bring peace to others.
Thomas à Kempis

Mercy unto you, and peace, and love, be multiplied.
Jude 1:2

Thou wilt keep him in perfect peace, whose mind is stayed on thee: because he trusteth in thee.

Isaiah 26:3

Now the God of hope fill you with all joy and peace in believing.

Romans 15:13

A dog never demands an explanation, requests an apology, or holds a grudge. A dog never ignores a proffered hand, refuses an honest heart, or withholds his boundless love. It's no wonder a dog is so easy to love in return!

Unconditional Love

We would not want to experience life without love! Yet we often limit the love we're prepared to give, perhaps because we have been hurt in the past, or we're afraid our love will be rejected.

God is love. No matter what your response to Him has been in the past, He loves you without limit, without hesitation, and without reservation. As the essence of pure love, He cannot do anything other than pour out His love to you.

Let Him refresh you and renew you in the pool of His infinite love.

Without reservation, dear God, I open my heart to Your love.
Amen

God is love.
1 John 4:8

*Because your love is better than life, my
lips will glorify you.*
Psalm 63:3 NIV

God is a light that is never darkened.
Francis Quarles

We love him, because he first loved us.
1 John 4:19

Love should be as natural
as living and breathing.
Mother Teresa

*The soul can split the sky in two and let
the face of God shine through.*
Edna St. Vincent Millay

If we love one another, God dwelleth
in us, and his love is perfected in us.
1 John 4:12

Love is a fruit in season at all times, and within reach of every hand.

Mother Teresa

The conclusion is always the same: love is the most powerful and still the most unknown energy of the world.

Teilhard de Chardin

A dog stands watchful, ready to sound the alarm at the whiff of a foreign scent or the sound of unfamiliar footsteps. Ears at the ready, she scans her territory, alert for dangers that could intrude on the peace and safety of her household.

Make a Difference

Most of us hurry through our day, too busy to stop and see the needs of others. We miss a chance to help...an opportunity to encourage...an opening to lift the burden on someone's heart simply because we aren't watching.

Today, keep an eye out for ways you can extend God's love to others. It might be something as silent as a smile or as fleeting as a warm hello...but it's something that could make a world of difference in someone's day.

Dear God, help me see the ways I can make a difference. Amen

The tissue of life to be
we weave with colors all our own,
And in the field of destiny
we reap as we have sown.

John Greenleaf Whittier

*Do to others what you would have them
do to you.*

Matthew 7:12 NIV

In all things showing yourself to be a
pattern of good works.

Titus 2:7

*You cannot always have happiness,
but you can always give happiness.*

Author Unknown

Let your light so shine before men,
that they may see your good works,
and glorify your Father which is
in heaven.

Matthew 5:16

If I can stop one heart from breaking,

I shall not live in vain;

If I can ease one life the aching,

Or cool one pain,

Or help one fainting robin

Unto his nest again,

I shall not live in vain.

Emily Dickinson

A dog seems to possess a sixth sense that picks up on human hurt and despondency, heartbreak and pain. His eyes peer beneath a facade of normalcy, and his affectionate nuzzles offer comfort and solace. It's hard not to think he understands everything.

Beneath the Mask

Before God, you need never hide your feelings or mask your true thoughts, no matter what they may look like. After all, He can see what's in your heart, and He knows you better than anyone else, sometimes even better than you know yourself.

Let God's kindly gaze search your heart and mind, and then receive the quiet comfort and compassion He offers you in mercy and love. There's nothing to hide— He truly understands it all.

Thank You, God, for understanding what I'm going through.
      Amen

Judge not according to the appearance,
but judge righteous judgment.
John 7:24

What lies behind us and what lies before us are
tiny matters compared to what lies within us.
Ralph Waldo Emerson

A man of understanding hath wisdom.
Proverbs 10:23

People look at the outward appearance,
but the LORD looks at the heart.
1 Samuel 16:7 NIV

It is only with the heart that one can see
rightly; what is essential is invisible to the eye.
Antoine de Saint-Exupéry

When we know how to read our own hearts,
we acquire wisdom of the hearts of others.
Denis Diderot

He that does good to another
does good also to himself.
Seneca

Recollect that the Almighty, who
gave the dog to be companion of
our pleasures and our toils, hath
invested him with a nature noble
and incapable of deceit.

Sir Walter Scott

One reason a dog can be such a
comfort when you're feeling blue is
that he doesn't try to find out why.

Author Unknown

As soon as the building pops into view, your dog makes herself as small as she can in her car seat. Maybe if she doesn't make a sound, you'll pass it right on by. Or maybe you'll forget about the appointment you made last week. But no such luck today. You park right under the sign: Main Street Animal Hospital and Veterinary Care.

Place of Healing

*Not every wound is visible on the outside.
For many of us, emotional wounds are deep
and take years to heal, if they heal at all.
There will always be a tender spot, painful
to the touch of a memory, a flashback, a
reminder of what happened so long ago.*

*These are the kinds of wounds God
alone can heal. He is your Great Physician,
willing and able to bring His comfort to your
spirit and of His compassion to your soul.*

*God's place of healing is wherever you
are hurting.*

Dear God, reach
Your healing hand
out to me.
      Amen

O LORD my God, I cried unto thee,
and thou hast healed me.
Psalm 30:2

The tasks are done and the tears are shed.
Yesterday's errors let yesterday cover;
Yesterday's wounds, which smarted and bled,
Are healed with the healing that night has shed.
Sarah Chauncey Woolsey

For you who revere my name, the sun of
righteousness will rise with healing in its rays.
Malachi 4:2 NIV

A wounded deer leaps the highest.
Emily Dickinson

They that are whole need not a physician;
but they that are sick.
Luke 5:31

He healeth the broken in heart,
and bindeth up their wounds.
Psalm 147:3

Character cannot be developed
in ease and quiet. Only through
experience of trial and suffering
can the soul be strengthened,
vision cleared, ambition inspired,
and success achieved.

Helen Keller

It's never same-old,
same-old with a dog.
She greets her yard
afresh each morning,
and she explores her
neighborhood with
expectation on the tip
of her nose each day.
On the scent for
excitement, she's sure
to find it!

Daily Miracles

The rosy horizon of a bright, clear morning...light and shadow waltzing the afternoon away...swatches of red and orange splashed across the sky in the evening...a canopy of stars at night. Have you ever stopped to think what miracles 24 hours bring?

When God created the world, He put His best work out for all the world to see, rich and poor alike. Spectacular miracles are yours for discovering (and for enjoying) every day of your life.

Dear God, open my
eyes to the miracle
of this day.
Amen

The real voyage of discovery consists not in
seeking new landscapes but in having new eyes.
Marcel Proust

For every house is builded by some man;
but he that built all things is God.
Hebrews 3:4

Were there no God, we would be in this glorious
world with grateful hearts: and no one to thank.
Christina Rossetti

In the beginning God created
the heaven and the earth.
Genesis 1:1

Write it on your heart that every day
is the best day in the year.
Ralph Waldo Emerson

He hath made the earth by his power, he hath
established the world by his wisdom, and hath
stretched out the heaven by his understanding.
Jeremiah 51:15

To me every hour of the light and dark is a
miracle. Every cubic inch of space is a miracle.
Walt Whitman

The soul should always stand ajar,
ready to welcome the ecstatic experience.
Emily Dickinson

I will praise thee; for I am fearfully and wonderfully made: marvellous are thy works; and that my soul knoweth right well.

Psalm 139:14

Sunshine is delicious, rain is refreshing, wind braces us up, snow is exhilarating; there is really no such thing as bad weather, only different kinds of good weather.

John Ruskin

Nobody is bored when he is trying to make something that is beautiful or to discover something that is true.

William Ralph Inge

Good, honest friendship comes naturally to a dog. With him, what you see is what you get— he has nothing to hide. And he has no reservations when it comes to meeting you, and after he does, his forever-love is yours for no other reason than because you're you.

The Art of Friendship

Attraction may happen instantly, but friendship between people needs time to grow and strengthen. It is cultivated with sincere interest in another's thoughts and feelings, and nurtured in shared experiences, celebrations, sorrows, and joys. When friendship blossoms, its beauty lasts a lifetime.

Your friendship with God takes time, too. Give yourself time to discover His plans and purpose for you, to deepen your understanding of His ways, and to grow in appreciation and love for Him.

When this friendship blossoms, its beauty lasts forever.

Nurture, dear God, the friendship I have found in You. Amen

FIRST FRIEND

When the Man waked up he said,
"What is Wild Dog doing here?"
And the Woman said,
"His name is not Wild Dog any more,
but the First Friend,
because he will be our friend
for always and always and always."
Rudyard Kipling

I have called you friends.
John 15:15

Abraham believed God...and he was
called the Friend of God.
James 2:23

A friend loveth at all times.
Proverbs 17:17

Our chief want in life is somebody
who can make us do what we can.
This is the service of a friend.
Ralph Waldo Emerson

As iron sharpens iron,
so one person sharpens another.
Proverbs 27:17 NIV

A friend is someone who knows you as you are, understands where you've been, accepts what you've become and still gently invites you to grow.

Author Unknown

Friendship is a sheltering tree.

Samuel Taylor Coleridge

Perhaps the most delightful friendships are those in which there is much agreement, much disputation, and yet more personal liking.

George Eliot

A dog's loyalty is legendary, and for good reason. He'll stick with you through thick and thin, and he doesn't give a yip for how rich or poor you are, or what kind of car you drive, or whether or not you aced your test or landed another promotion. All that matters to him is being there with you.

Always Faithful

God's faithfulness to you goes beyond anything you have ever experienced. Even if you find yourself pushed to the extremes of hardship or engulfed in the most tangled of difficulties, He asks no prying questions, and offers no judgmental comments.

Even if you have not always been faithful to God, He still remains faithful to you. What matters to Him is not your past or present situation—all that matters to Him is you.

Dear God,
no matter where
I am in my life,
Your faithfulness
never fails!
　　　Amen

The Lord is faithful
who shall stablish you.
2 Thessalonians 3:3

*Thy counsels of old are faithfulness
and truth.*
Isaiah 25:1

Nothing is more noble, nothing more
venerable than fidelity. Faithfulness
and truth are the most sacred excellences
and endowments of the human mind.
Cicero

*Let love and faithfulness never leave you;
bind them around your neck, write them on
the tablet of your heart.*
Proverbs 3:3 NIV

I will never leave thee, nor forsake thee.
Hebrews 13:5

This God is our God for ever and ever.
Psalm 48:14

Faith is the virtue by which,
clinging-to the faithfulness
of God, we lean upon him,
so that we may obtain what
he gives to us.

William Ames

The LORD will not cast off his
people, neither will he forsake
his inheritance.

Psalm 94:14

Sometimes a stray dog just appears at the door. He looks up, drawing our sympathy with his big, pleading eyes. We don't know where he's been or where he comes from, but after one bowl of food and a pat on the head, we open the door and let him come in.

Where You Belong

Your story began at the beginning of time when God called you to be His own. Before you were born, He knew your name. He planned your life to have a purpose, and He promised to be with you every step of the way.

No matter where you are now in the story of your life, God invites you to put your hand in His. Nothing has changed from the beginning. His door is always open for you.

Dear God,
thank you for
giving me a place
where I belong—
with You.
Amen

Before I was born the LORD called me;
from my mother's womb he has spoken my name.
Isaiah 49:1 NIV

A mysterious bond of brotherhood
makes all men one.
Thomas Carlyle

Ye are the children of the LORD your God.
Deuteronomy 14:1

He is our God; and we are the people
of his pasture, and the sheep of his hand.
Psalm 95:7

Be ye therefore followers of God, as dear children.
Ephesians 5:1

The Father most tender, Father of all,
my immense God—I His atom.
Elizabeth Ann Seton

When we lose God, it is not God who is lost.
Author Unknown

Ye are the temple of the living God;
as God hath said, I will dwell in them,
and walk in them; and I will be their
God, and they shall be my people.

2 Corinthians 6:16

The light of God surrounds me;
The love of God enfolds me;
The power of God protects me;
The presence of God watches over me.
Wherever I am, God is.

James Dillet Freeman

All you have to do is pick up your keys and head to the car, and she's right there beside you...ahead of you... jumping at the door of the car in anticipation of another glorious outing. To the grocery store? The park? The beach? It doesn't matter, as long as she gets to ride along!

Be Happy

Who is happy? Those who can appreciate the wonder of a new day, go about routine activities with mindfulness and enthusiasm, and enjoy the companionship of those around them have what it takes to be truly happy.

Happiness is a willingness to embrace the day, knowing that, whatever it may bring, you have a steady companion in your loving God. With Him, you have everything you need to be happy...and to bring happiness to others.

Grant me, dear God, the gift of true happiness.
Amen

Happy is the man that findeth wisdom,
and the man that getteth understanding.
Proverbs 3:13

*To live is so startling it leaves little time
for anything else.*
Emily Dickinson

You give them drink
from your river of delights.
Psalm 36:8 NIV

I delight to do thy will, O my God.
Psalm 40:8

We...rejoice in hope of the glory of God.
Romans 5:2

The right to happiness is fundamental.
Anna Pavlova

Happy is that people, whose God is the LORD.
Psalm 144:15

My soul shall be joyful in the LORD.
Psalm 35:9

Enthusiasm gives life to what is invisible;
and interest to what has no immediate action
on our comfort in this world.
Madame de Stael

Men are made for happiness, and
anyone who is completely happy
has a right to say to himself: "I am
doing God's will on earth."

Anton Chekhov

The gloom of the world is but a
shadow, behind it, yet within reach
is joy, there is radiance and glory
in the darkness could we but see
and to see we have only to look.

Fra Giovanni

There is no duty we so much
underrate as the duty of being
happy.

Robert Louis Stevenson

Your dog depends on you to meet his needs, for you are the sole source of his food, shelter, and happiness. When he looks up at you with pleading, expectant eyes, what else can you do but respond with generous love—love to last a lifetime and beyond!

Believe in Prayer

Prayers lift up our thoughts, needs, and desires to God. So often, however, we let our words dangle somewhere between earth and heaven, wondering if God has any interest in hearing them.

It is your conviction of faith and your confidence in His goodness that gives substance to your prayers. Pray, believing your Father is willing and able to grant your requests, and then await His answer.

How it comes could surprise you, so open your eyes and your ears...and your heart!

Dear God,
please hear me
when I pray.
Amen

Ask, and it shall be given you;
seek, and ye shall find; knock,
and it shall be opened unto you.
Matthew 7:7

Prayer is the contemplation of the facts
of life from the highest point of view.
Ralph Waldo Emerson

More things are wrought by prayer
than this world dreams of.
Alfred Lord Tennyson

In every thing by prayer and supplication
with thanksgiving let your
requests be made known unto God.
Philippians 4:6

What things soever ye desire,
when ye pray, believe that ye receive them,
and ye shall have them.
Mark 11:24

Pray in the Spirit on all occasions
with all kinds of prayers and requests.
Ephesians 6:18 NIV

Direct all your prayers to one thing only, that is, to conform your will perfectly to the Divine Will.

Teresa of Avila

Pray without ceasing.

1 Thessalonians 5:17

Where's that noise coming from on this dark night? Her ears perk up, her muzzle lifts, her whole being tenses in high alert as she awaits the next telltale clue. As soon as it comes, she quickly gets up and bravely leads you to its source—a tree branch brushing across the window in the wind.

Take Courage

Heroes are men and women who perform great acts of courage in trying circumstances—and heroes are people like you.

It takes courage to face life's letdowns and disappointments, its sorrows and setbacks. It takes courage to identify the source of personal problems and work to overcome them; to hold to principle in the midst of challenges; and to remain positive when things aren't going your way.

Real heroes, though, never go it alone. Real heroes go with God.

Stay with me, dear God, as I face the challenges of my day.
Amen

The LORD is the strength of my life;
of whom shall I be afraid?
Psalm 27:1

Be strong and of a good courage;
be not afraid, neither be thou dismayed:
for the LORD thy God is with thee
whithersoever thou goest.
Joshua 1:9

Courage is resistance to fear,
mastery of fear, not absence of fear.
Mark Twain

Wait on the LORD: be of good courage,
and he shall strengthen thine heart:
wait, I say, on the LORD.
Psalm 27:14

You must do the thing
you think you cannot do.
Eleanor Roosevelt

Let not your heart be troubled,
neither let it be afraid.
John 14:27

In times of stress, be bold and valiant.
Horace

Courage is the greatest of all
virtues, because if you haven't
courage, you may not have an
opportunity to use any of
the others.

Samuel Johnson

Jesus spake unto them, saying,
Be of good cheer; it is I;
be not afraid.

Matthew 14:27

Be of good courage, and he shall
strengthen your heart, all ye that
hope in the LORD.

Psalm 31:24

Early training is vital to a dog's well-being. Through training, a dog learns household manners and develops social skills, preparing him to fit into the family and bond with his humans. The well-trained dog looks to his human to show him how, and he wouldn't have it any other way!

Setting an Example

In all probability, you influence others more than you realize. The words you speak shape how people respond to you, and the things you do have an effect on how people perceive you. Your opinions can sway others, and the way you live your life can inspire others.

Think of yourself as a leader, because that is what you are. Lead others to find confidence by encouraging their efforts... to discover self-worth by highlighting their strengths...to discover God's love by seeing it reflected in you.

God,
help me influence
others for the good.
Amen

I have given you an example,
that ye should do as I have done to you.
John 13:15

Ye are the light of the world.
A city that is set on an hill cannot be hid.
Matthew 5:14

My advice is to consult the lives of other men,
as we would a looking glass, and from thence
fetch examples of our own imitation.
Terence

It is no use walking anywhere to preach
unless our walking is our preaching.
Francis of Assisi

What do we live for, if it is not to make life less
difficult for each other?
George Eliot

I am satisfied, that we are less convinced
by what we hear than by what we see.
Herodotus

Be thou an example of the
believers, in word, in conversation,
in charity, in spirit, in faith,
in purity.

1 Timothy 4:12

Let us preach you without
preaching, not by words but by
our example, by the catching force,
the sympathetic influence of what
we do.

John Henry Newman

A dog has a way of
making you feel that
you're the smartest,
funniest, most lovable
person in the whole
wide world—because
in her eyes, you are!

God's Approval

Early on, you probably were taught to work for what you wanted—and that's excellent advice, except when it comes to God's approval. There's nothing you need to do to earn His approval! Why? Because you already have it.

His affection and compassion for you remain the same, no matter who you are or where you are. It's something you can't earn, and it's something you're not asked to earn, so you can relax.

Look to Him, and you will find His approval there waiting for you.

Dear God,
help me embrace
everything that Your
approval means.
Amen

*It is not the one who commends himself
who is approved, but the one whom
the Lord commends.*
2 Corinthians 10:18 NIV

We learn that God is, that he is in me,
and that all things are shadows of Him.
Ralph Waldo Emerson

*God saw every thing that he had made,
and, behold, it was very good.*
Genesis 1:31

We are, in the hands of God,
like blocks of marble in the hands
of sculptors.
Alphonsus Liguori

*We should ask nothing and refuse
nothing, but leave ourselves in the arms
of Divine Providence without wasting
time in any desire, except to will
what God wills of us.*
Francis de Sales

Let us remember that within us there is a palace of immense magnificence.

Teresa of Avila

Your dog makes no plans, because she trusts you to take care of her needs tomorrow as you have today. She worries not at all what will happen to her, because she relies on you to be there for her in the future as you are at this moment. She lives unburdened by care, because she knows she belongs to you.

A Worry-Free Life

When you trust in God to take care of your tomorrows, here's how it affects today: you can live free of worry about the future.

Dependence on Him to be there for you in the future allows you to make the most of the day you have right now—which, in turn, shapes and strengthens your ability to handle whatever the future may bring!

Live fully today, and leave the future (and forever) in His hands.

Keep me always, dear God, in Your hands.
        Amen

Can any one of you by worrying
add a single hour to your life?
Matthew 6:27 NIV

When speculation has done its worst,
two and two still make four.
Samuel Johnson

Do not worry about tomorrow,
for tomorrow will worry about itself.
Each day has enough trouble of its own.
Matthew 6:34 NIV

A hundredload of worry will not pay
an ounce of debt.
George Herbert

Do not be anxious about anything, but in
every situation, by prayer and petition, with
thanksgiving, present your requests to God.
Philippians 4:6 NIV

Casting all your care upon him;
for he careth for you.
1 Peter 5:7

Seek not ye what ye shall eat, or what ye
shall drink, neither be ye of doubtful mind.
Luke 12:29

Worry never climbed a hill,

Worry never paid a bill,

Worry never dried a tear,

Worry never calmed a fear...

Worry never darned a heel,

Worry never cooked a meal,

It never led a horse to water...

nor ever did a thing it oughter!

Anonymous

Most dogs relish playing tug-of-war, a game of strength and perseverance. The game provides good exercise for the dog, and it's also an opportunity for the dog's human "opponent" to establish rules, teach obedience, and insist on acceptable behavior during play.

Give and Take

You probably know someone who approaches life as a tug-of-war, someone who plays to win at all costs. Perhaps at one time you found yourself in a tug-of-war with someone, and you definitely didn't want to lose!

When a tug-of-war contest gives way to a give-and-take attitude, however, there are winners all around. Reason tells you that you aren't able to take the trophy home every time; and God's Spirit persuades you that you don't need to.

In God, humbly take...and cheerfully give.

Dear God,
teach me when to
hold on tight to
what is important...
and when to give.
Amen

He who stays not in his littleness,
loses his greatness.
Francis de Sales

Be completely humble and gentle; be patient,
bearing with one another in love.
Ephesians 4:2 NIV

God gives us always strength enough, and sense
enough, for everything He wants us to do.
John Ruskin

God loveth a cheerful giver.
2 Corinthians 9:7

Our energy is in proportion to the resistance
it meets. We can attempt nothing great, but from
a sense of the difficulties we have to encounter.
William Hazlitt

Finite to fail, but infinite to venture.
Emily Dickinson

For thou, LORD, hast made me glad
through thy work:
I will triumph in the works of thy hands.
Psalm 92:4

A time to get, and a time to lose;

a time to keep, and a time to cast away;

A time to rend, and a time to sew;

a time to keep silence, and a time to speak;

A time to love, and a time to hate;

a time of war, and a time of peace.

Ecclesiastes 3:6-8

Throw the stick, and he bounds across the lawn to fetch it, grabbing it in his teeth without missing a beat, circling in a great U-turn, and bringing it back again. You throw the stick...and the scene would repeat for eternity if you didn't call at the end of one last throw, "Come on—it's time to go in!"

Keep At It

More and more we're becoming accustomed to getting what we want the instant we want it. Yet many things—and most worthwhile things—still take time.

Achievement of a worthy goal...healing of body or spirit...attainment of expertise in your field...deepening of love between you and another...heightening appreciation of God's presence in your life...all these things take time.

Do not let go. Keep at it.

Help me persevere,
Father, in my good
work.
      Amen

Ye have need of patience, that,
after ye have done the will of God,
ye might receive the promise.
Hebrews 10:36

Blessed is the man who perseveres under trial.
James 1:12 NIV

In the realm of ideas everything depends
on enthusiasm; in the real world,
all rests on perseverance.
Johann von Goethe

Let us run with patience
the race that is set before us.
Hebrews 12:1

The heights by great men reached and kept
were not attained by sudden flight,
but they, while their companions slept
were toiling upward in the night.
Henry Wadsworth Longfellow

Let us not be weary in well doing: for in
due season we shall reap, if we faint not.
Galatians 6:9

Remember, no effort that we make
to attain something beautiful is ever lost.
Helen Keller

We count them happy which endure.
James 5:11

Nothing in the world can take
the place of Persistence. Talent
will not; nothing is more common
than unsuccessful men with talent.
Genius will not; unrewarded genius
is almost a proverb.
Education will not; the world
is full of educated derelicts.
Persistence and determination
alone are omnipotent.

Calvin Coolidge

Discover the joy of having a dog companion by finding activities you and your dog can do together. Play with him, cuddle with him, take him for walks around the neighborhood, and bring him along on dog-friendly trips. The more time you spend together, the stronger the bond between you grows, and the more rewards you both enjoy.

True Joy

Joy is one of God's many gifts to you. Unlike happiness, which depends on feelings and circumstances, joy is a spiritual constant. More than a feeling, it is an attitude of being; more than what's going on around you, it's what's going on inside you.

Your joy of spirit is expressed in your ability to see the good in hardship, and to find fulfillment in your work, hobbies, and relationships. It's evident in the positive feelings you bring to others every day through your words and actions.

Be joyous…and share the joy.

Dear God,
grant me the gift
of true joy.
Amen

Rejoice in the Lord alway:
and again I say, Rejoice.
Philippians 4:4

Joy is an elation of spirit —
of a spirit that trusts in the goodness
and truth of its own possessions.
Seneca

To get the full value from joy you must
have someone to divide it with.
Mark Twain

Thou hast put gladness in my heart.
Psalm 4:7

Our heart shall rejoice in him, because
we have trusted in his holy name.
Psalm 33:21

Where there is joy and poverty,
there is neither greed nor avarice.
Francis of Assisi

Who is the happiest of men?

He who values the merits of others,

and in their pleasure takes joy,

even as though t'were his own.

Johann von Goethe

You give your dog everything she needs, and more. Not just a bowl of food, but tasty treats to reward her stellar behavior...not simply a walk down the street, but a romp of tennis balls and disks in the backyard...not merely a pat on the head, but a big, warm hug at the end of the day.

Blessing of Abundance

If you have spent time counting your blessings lately, you quickly came to the conclusion that God has given you not only what you need, and more! He has provided for your basic needs, and He has added... what? Perhaps good health...loved ones... longtime friends...fulfilling work... a captivating hobby...a comfortable home... a refrigerator full of delicious meals...

What do you need? Ask Him. Then thank Him for the abundance you already possess.

Thank You,
Father, for Your
abundant blessings.
Amen

Abundance consists not so much in
material possessions, but in an
uncovetous spirit.
John Selden

*They feast on the abundance of
your house; you give them drink
from your river of delights.*
Psalm 36:8 NIV

If we fasten our attention on what we
have, rather than what we lack,
a very little wealth is sufficient.
Francis Johnson

*I know there are no errors,
In the great Eternal plan,
And all things work together
For the final good of man.*
Ella Wheeler Wilcox

He brought me forth also into
a large place: he delivered me,
because he delighted in me.
2 Samuel 22:20

Whosoever hath, to him shall be given, and he shall have more abundance.

Matthew 13:12

The man who thinks his wife, his baby, his house, his horse, his dog, and himself severely unequalled, is almost sure to be a good-humored person.

Oliver Wendell Holmes

One dog walks in a mannered trot, his leash lax in the hand of his companion. The other dog yanks the leash taut, attracted by a squirrel here, a butterfly there, a swirl of leaves in the distance. Her companion is constantly pulling this dog out of the line of danger, aching arm notwithstanding!

Secure in Him

From time to time, temptation lures us to those places God would have us avoid. Danger! our conscience whispers as God's Spirit nudges us back on His path. Through Scripture and the counsel of spiritual friends, we recieve words to help us keep on track.

God doesn't keep you on a leash, and has given you freedom of choice. But know that He is there to pull you back from anything that would threaten your relationship with Him.

Dear God,
help me return to
Your path when I am
tempted to stray.
Amen

When opportunity for self-surrender arises,
seize it. You will discover the secret in what
you had hitherto tried to avoid; indeed,
you will find even more.

Thomas à Kempis

*When water surrenders to the flow
of the river it reaches the ocean, so also must
we surrender in order to reach our Source.*

Author Unknown

Create in me a clean heart, O God;
and renew a right spirit within me.

Psalm 51:10

*Be not conformed to this world: but be ye
transformed by the renewing of your mind,
that ye may prove what is that good,
and acceptable, and perfect, will of God.*

Romans 12:2

He restoreth my soul: he leadeth me in the
paths of righteousness for his name's sake.

Psalm 23:3

We must follow, not force providence.

William Shakespeare

The great thing is to resign all
your interests and pleasures and
comfort and fame to God. He who
unreservedly accepts whatever
God may give him in this world—
humiliation, trouble and trial from
within or from without—has made
a great step towards self-victory.

Francois Fenelon

Be renewed in the spirit of
your mind.

Ephesians 4:23

A great day is every day he wakes up, greets his human companion, takes his breakfast, explores the yard, and watches the neighbor's kids leave for school. Then he vigilantly guards the house until the afternoon wanes, his companion returns, his bowl refilled; as the evening wears on, everyone settles down to a cozy, contented rest.

Priorities In Order

If you want to check your priorities, open your daily planner and page through your list of to-do's, appointments, activities, and errands. Are you surprised?

God invites you to put Him first—first in your thoughts, first in your attention, first in your day. When your priority is Him, everything else has a way of falling right into place. Everything—all the to-do's, appointments, activities, and errands. Try it—you'll be really surprised how well it works!

Dear God,
let me set my heart
and mind, my
time and energy,
towards what is
important.
　　　Amen

Seek ye first the kingdom of God,
and his righteousness; and all these things
shall be added unto you.
Matthew 6:33

Thou shalt have no other gods before me.
Exodus 20:3

What's the use of running
when you're on the wrong road?
German Proverb

Far away in the sunshine are my highest
aspirations. I may not reach them, but I can look
up and see their beauty, believe in them, and try
to follow where they lead.
Louisa May Alcott

We look not at the things which are seen, but
at the things which are not seen: for the things
which are seen are temporal; but the things
which are not seen are eternal.
2 Corinthians 4:18

Nothing contributes so much to tranquilize
the mind as a steady purpose—a point on which
the soul may fix its intellectual eye.
Mary Wollstonecraft Shelley

Keep in mind that you are always saying "no" to something. If it isn't to the apparent, urgent things in your life, it is probably to the most fundamental, highly important things. Even when the urgent is good, the good can keep you from your best, keep you from your unique contribution, if you let it.

Helen Keller

You identify your dog's bark, whether it's coming from around the block or from the middle of a crowded dog park. In the same way, you can tell the sound of one neighbor's lab from another's dachshund, and of your friend's shepherd from a stray terrier. Like our human voices, each bark is unique to its owner.

Sound of His Voice

As you grow in your relationship with God, you become more and more familiar with the sound of His voice in your life. You hear His words of comfort when you're down, and you discern His wise counsel when you have questions.

His voice is distinctive; what He says lifts, renews, and restores you. His words fill your heart with the encouragement you need to hear, and in the sound of His voice, you discover your security and safety.

Listen...above all others, hear His voice.

Speak to me,
dear God, so I may
listen to Your words.
Amen

My sheep hear my voice,
and I know them, and they follow me.
John 10:27

Speak, LORD; for thy servant heareth.
1 Samuel 3:9

Nothing gives rest but the sincere
search for truth.
Blaise Pascal

To day if ye will hear his voice,
harden not your hearts.
Hebrews 4:7

The geat blessings of mankind are
within us and within our reach;
but we shut our eyes, and like people
in the dark, we fall foul upon the very
thing we search for, without finding it.
Seneca

Be still, and know that I am God.
Psalm 46:10

There is guidance for each of us,
and by lowly listening we shall hear
the right word.
Ralph Waldo Emerson

The mighty God, even the LORD,

hath spoken, and called the earth

from the rising of the sun unto

the going down thereof.

Psalm 50:1

Bless Them All, Dear Lord

Hear our prayer, Lord,
for all animals;
May they be well-fed
and well-treated and happy;
Protect them from hunger
and fear and suffering.

Especially bless, dear God,
the special dog with such
great devotion, who gives us
the gifts of love, loyalty
and friendship.

Amen

The End